Jadon Visits the Trout Pond

I0752576

with Mrs. Nita & Mr. Ron

By Carol Van Zanden

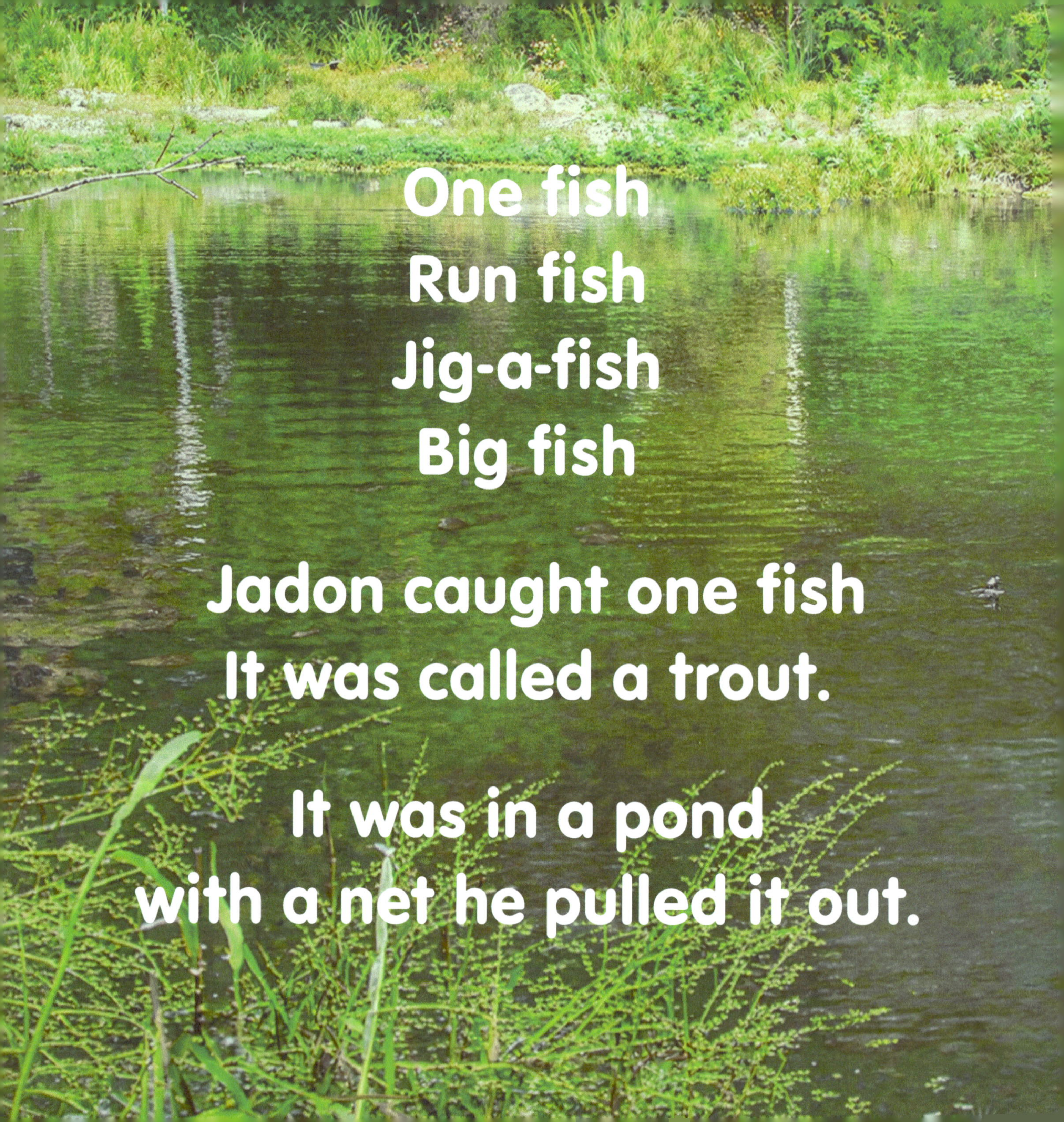

One fish
Run fish
Jig-a-fish
Big fish

Jadon caught one fish
It was called a trout.

It was in a pond
with a net he pulled it out.

Mr. Ron helped net it
because it looked so fierce.

The one fish was a Big one
The biggest trout this year.

Mrs. Nita cooked it
She put it in the oven.

It looked so good and tasty
he could eat a dozen!

First, we make the dog food sticky with water.

Now the bait is on the hook.

Be careful.
Don't lose the bait!

You can try casting, Jadon.

Good job!
You missed my line.

I think this is the right way

Yes, turn the reel slowly.

It's a big one!

Let me help you so the trout doesn't get away.

Wow! It's the biggest trout caught this year.

Get the net, Jadon!

We netted it!

Is the fish stuck in the net?

No, we caught it!

THE END

Mrs. Nita cooked the trout.
It was yummy!

Garlic Butter Trout in Foil

1 pound trout fillet, skin side down
2 tablespoons Butter
1 tsp Parsley, minced
Salt and pepper to taste

1. Preheat oven to 375F.

2. Rub piece of aluminum foil with oil. Place the trout fillet in the center and fold up the sides of the foil. Season trout with lemon juice, salt and pepper.

3. Melt butter, stir in fresh minced garlic and drizzle over the trout.

4. Create a closed packet around the fish. Fold the foil sides over it. Place foil pack on oven rack and bake until cooked through, about 15-20 minutes.

5. For a browned top, open the foil slightly and broil for the last 5 minutes.

Mrs. Nita and Mr. Ron, 

Thanks for letting us come. I liked about fishing and I catched a bigger fish than Mr. Ron–kind of. The sunset is like you made but a little beautiful.

Thank you,
Jadon

Special Thanks

Jadon, Mr. Ron, Mrs. Nita and Britt Sekulic

popstradamus.com

Paperback ISBN: 979-8-9916273-8-2

Book design by Britt Sekulic

© 2026 Copyright Carol Van Zanden. All rights reserved.

About the Author

Carol Van Zanden is a retired Home Economics and kindergarten teacher who has lived in the Pacific Northwest all her life. With her BA and MA in Education, her 38-year professional career encompassed teaching in early elementary, high school, college, and adult education. Mrs Nita was a part-time aide in Carol's kindergraten class for many years. Carol and her husband, Ted, raised their children in Oak Harbor, Washington.

Through the years, Carol combined her love of family and photography, capturing memories of their grandchildren's visits with her camera. Years ago, she cut and pasted a series of books together using photos of her granddaughter and grandson to be read to by their parents and written in early childhood language for them to read by themselves. Not knowing that someday her prayers would be answered, with the help of self-publishing and collaborating with a local bookmaker and friend, the books would be brought to life professionally for other parents to read to their children and for them to read themselves.

Did you enjoy this book?
Try another book in
the series:

Four and Twenty Blackberries
Baked in Jadon's Pie
By Carol Van Zanden

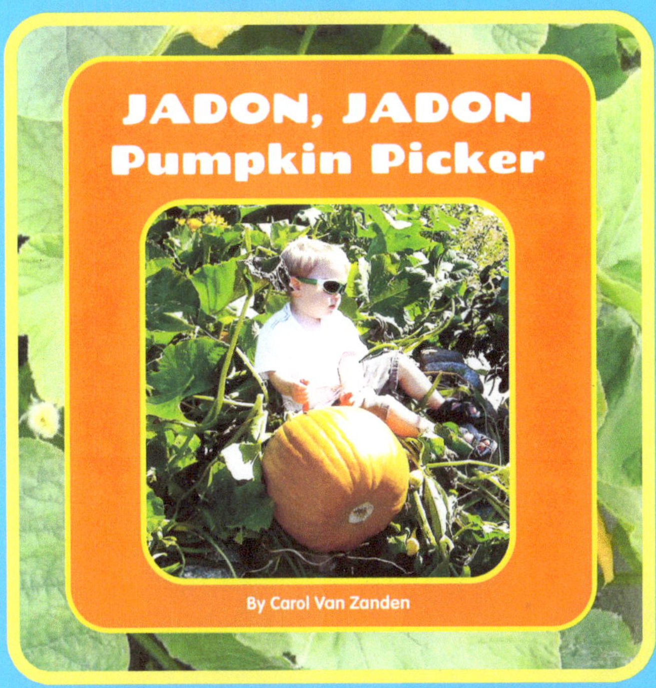
JADON, JADON
Pumpkin Picker
By Carol Van Zanden

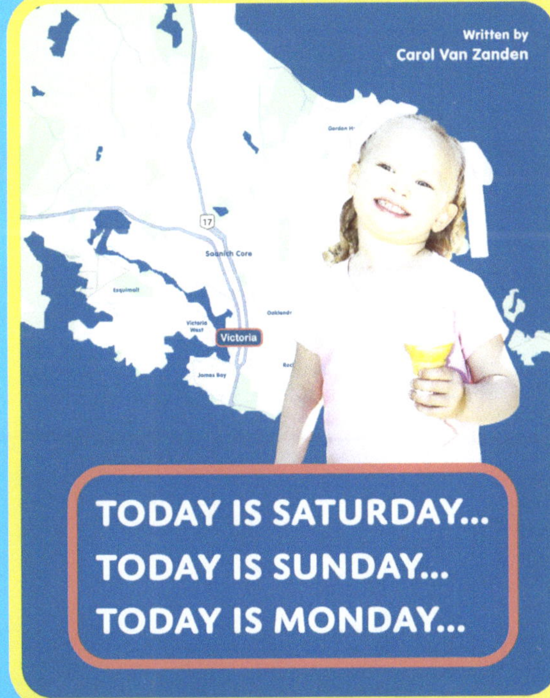
Written by
Carol Van Zanden
Victoria
TODAY IS SATURDAY...
TODAY IS SUNDAY...
TODAY IS MONDAY...

Jadon, Way Up High
in the Apple Tree
By Carol Van Zanden

www.ingramcontent.com/pod-product-compliance
Lightning Source LLC
LaVergne TN
LVHW070206110826
845147LV00002B/520

* 9 7 9 8 9 9 1 6 2 7 3 8 2 *